Advance Praise

"*SMART Women Create Membership-Based Businesses* teaches women why the business model they use is crucial to their success as an entrepreneur. Start with a powerful business model and you set yourself up for success."

—**Kim Fulcher**, CEO of My Life Compass and Author of *Remodel Your Reality*

"The road to a truly successful, lasting membership site can be a tricky one, and it pays (really pays) to get it right from the beginning. Sheri McConnell teaches you how to leverage and lead by using one of the most powerful formulas that exist: the membership-based business model."

—**Andrea J. Lee**, Award-Winning Author of *Multiple Streams of Coaching Income*

"Sheri McConnell empowers and teaches women to find *their people* and *bring them together* and to use *their intuitive power to achieve greatness*. Very SMART indeed."

—**Dan Poynter**, Author of *The Self-Publishing Manual*

"Whether you are dreaming about a membership-based business or are already running one, Sheri McConnell offers resources you've dreamed existed but didn't have time to find. She's put the resources together for you and presents them in the context of streamlining your path to success. How welcome!"

—**Sheila Bender**, Founder and Publisher of Writing It Real and Author of *Writing in a Convertible with the Top Down*

"Another trail-blazing book from a trail-blazer herself. Sheri has put together a comprehensive, helpful, and innovative guide to a truly successful business model for women everywhere!"

—**Penny C. Sansevieri**, CEO Author Marketing Experts, Inc and Author of *Red Hot Internet Publicity*

"Sheri's book is a wonderful guidebook that empowers women to create more abundance in their lives through the most powerful tool we have, connecting. The beauty of Sheri's model is that it's perfect for women who want to work from home and earn a great living following their passion. What could be better?"

—**Debbie LaChusa**, Founder and Owner of 6 Figure Work At Home Mom and 10 Step Marketing

"Everything you need to know for a plug and play membership site that will help thousands, fulfill your own life purpose and create a rich platform for online recognition. A genuinely useful guide for the woman entrepreneur."
—**Suzanne Falter-Barns**, Author of *How Much Joy* and
CEO of Get Known Now

"A simple, easy to understand guide that anyone can use to get started with a membership-based business!"
—**Alexandria Brown**, Online Entrepreneur and Millionaire
Marketing and Success Coach

"*Smart Women Create Membership-Based Businesses* is essential reading for any woman who wants to discover the power of leverage in their business model. With just one tip from this book full of golden nuggets, you'll be able to catapult your revenue and results forward light years. I personally have experienced an extra $100k in my bottom line from membership based businesses—I hope you will too!"
—**Melanie Benson Strick**, Million Dollar Lifestyle Business
Coach & Virtual Team Building Expert

"If you want the step-by-step system to creating membership sites the fulfilling, fun and profitable way, get this book now! Sheri doesn't just tell you what to do—she shows you every step of the way. She's the real deal!"
—**Stephanie Frank**, Best Selling Author of *Accidental Millionaire*

"Sheri McConnell's expertise cuts extensive amounts of time off your learning curve as she clearly defines how to create your own association. She deliberately walks you through every step with tried and true tips and tools that are proven. Following her instruction, you will meet with tremendous success.
—**Dotsie Bregel**, Founder of the National Association of
Baby Boomer Women and Boomer Women Speak

"*Smart Women Create Membership-Based Businesses* is a powerful resource for women entrepreneurs because it teaches them about the leverage they will have as the owner of membership-based business. Sheri's experience and those she interviewed further emphasizes the exponential power you have to do more with your life when you are using a business model that works for you."
—**Wendy Weiss**, The Queen of Cold Calling

"The power of leverage! Read this book to learn how to create a membership business and leverage all of your resources. You'll have more time, connections, energy, and money. You'll be a leader in your field. Best of all, you'll help more people and have more fun."
—**Larina Kase**, Author of *The Confident Leader*

"Sheri's *Smart Women Create Membership-Based Businesses* explains how it is possible to *have it all* if you want it. She shares her practical yet powerful 'attraction-based' business model to show women how they can build and run a profitable business from scratch while raising a family.
—**Brian Jud**, Author of *How To Make Real Money Selling Books* and *Beyond the Bookstore*

"*Celebrate your life* and learn how the membership-based business model lets you leverage your time, money, and expertise exponentially so that you have more free time to do what you enjoy."
—**Melissa Galt**, America's Lifestyle Diva and Author of *Celebrate Your Life*

"Sheri McConnell has been an amazing inspiration and is the sole reason why my own membership-based site exists today. *Smart Women Create Membership-Based Businesses* is perfect for female entrepreneurs who want to learn why the membership-based business is such a powerful business structure. You really can't afford not to have this book in your library!"
—**Erin Blaskie**, Co-Creator of Virtual Assistant Mastermind

"A smart and handy step-by-step approach for building successful membership sites. You'll get both the business model and the infrastructure to develop a long-term relationship with your members."
—**Barbara McRae**, Bestselling Author of *Coach Your Teen to Success*

"Sheri McConnell is a role model for any women in business. Listen to what she says and model what she does and you'll be on your way to a successful business. Her information on creating a membership-based business is what you need—now!"
—**Elizabeth Hagen**, Author of *Organize With Confidence*

"Following Buckminster Fuller's edict to 'do more with less,' Sheri has captured the magic of producing more results with less effort, while at the same time producing more wealth and more joy, in the easiest possible way – through organizing membership-based businesses. All entrepreneurs should make this a 'must-read' so they do not miss the opportunities Sheri outlines."
—**Pat Lynch**, CEO of Audio Acrobat and Women's Radio/Women's Calendar

"*Smart Women Create Membership-Based Businesses* is a terrific primer for teaching you how to create your new membership-based business. This really works! We tripled our membership while promoting our first virtual free event using her techniques. Sheri is sincere, warm, humorous, and really smart too!"
—**Linda Joy Myers**, President of the National Association of Memoir Writers and Author of *Don't Call Me Mother* and *Becoming Whole: Writing Your Healing Story*

"I'm so excited about this book! First, I love that a woman has written it. Second, I love that a woman with such an authentic voice and spirit has written it. There's wisdom in here for everyone from entrepreneurs to artists to service professionals. Sheri is showing the way to a life of courage, wealth, and inspiration."

—**Christine Kane**, Singer/Songwriter, Public Speaker, and
    Creativity Consultant

"This book is a must for women who want to create a more powerful business. Sheri shares an amazing business model with her readers, one that is so much smarter than most business models on the market today. True success is on the horizon for all who read and implement the model found in this inspiring book!"

— **Dahlynn McKowen**, Author of *Chicken Soup for the Soul*

"Sheri's step-by-step process of how to start a virtual membership-based business is right on track. She keeps the information clear, focused and easy enough for anyone to follow. I am currently recommending her process to my private coaching clients and members of our Smart Women community."

—**Katana Abbott**, CFP®, Founder of Smart Women Coaching

"*Smart Women Create Membership-Based Businesses* reveals a money-making business model that is the perfect fit for women entrepreneurs. I HIGHLY recommend this definitive guide if you're looking to break out of the time-for-dollars trap and create powerful, sustainable cash flow using your gifts!"

—**Kendall SummerHawk**, the "Horse Whisperer for Business" Author of
    Brilliance Unbridled and *How to Charge What You're Worth and Get It!*

"If there is one person I know who understand the value of developing a business model leveraging the creation of a membership programme and building a thriving community then it's Sheri McConnell. In this book Sheri lays out the foundations and steps to creating a membership based business. If you are looking for ways to build on your reputation, tap into a new profit stream and become a key influencer in your market place, then this book is a must read."

—**Krishna De**, Founder of Big Growth News

a few words from...
Smart Women Who Created Membership-Based Businesses

"Your sphere of influence multiplies many, many times over in terms of being able to have people that are very pleased with what you're doing and they actively want to be affiliated with you. They will help you reach out and do what you need to do. Maybe not in the volunteer way but certainly in making more introductions and helping you increase your sphere of influence."
—**Leslie Grossman**, President of the Women's Leadership Exchange

"I'm very comfortable contacting someone who I don't know but who I know of simply because I do have a platform that I can reference that lends immediate credibility. They may not be interested in what I'm proposing or what I'm offering but nine times out of ten, I will always get the call because I can say, 'Check out my online community.'"
—**Kim Fulcher**, CEO of My Life Compass

"We are the gatekeeper to the direct sellers, the people in this profession. And other people are recognizing that if they want to reach this marketplace, then they want to come to us."
—**Nicki Keohohou**, President of the Direct Women's Selling Alliance

"When you have an association, you have an immediate platform."
—**Dotsie Bregel**, President of the National Association
   of Baby Boomer Women

"People are going to view you as a leader in your industry. You're going to have to create innovative solutions. People are going to look up to you. People are going to want to be around you, mastermind with you, and that's huge. The results that stem from running an association, all the products, programs, events, joint venture partnerships that I'm able to pull together, that has taken me well into six figures. I took a gigantic leap thanks to the association."
—**Milana Leshinsky**, President of the Association of Coaching and
   Consulting Professionals on the Web

"The membership-based business model has afforded me the unique platform to network and partner with top leaders in my industry, help students around the world, and empower myself with the tools to make money leveraging my skills and passions. Every time a student tells me how Campus Calm is changing their life for the better, I am reminded that the membership-based business model is so much bigger than just me reshaping my life. I get to live

my dream and change the world at the same time. I'm so honored and humbled. Thank you Sheri for empowering me with the mindsets to change my life and give back to the world!"
—**Maria Pascucci**, President & Founder of Campus Calm

"As an owner of a membership site myself, I can tell you that *Smart Women Create Membership-Based Businesses* exposes the truth of why a membership-based business model is so powerful—especially for female entrepreneurs. Beyond a great business model, my membership site has brought me so much closer to my community of entrepreneurs and we all work together to help each other succeed—and that is the best reward."
—**Stefanie Hartman**, CEO SHE Inc. and Founder of Millionaires
In Training (MIT) Program and the PrivateJVClub.com

THE *Smart Women* SERIES™

Smart Women
Create
Membership-Based
Businesses

Sheri McConnell

President and Founder
of
National Association of Women Writers
Association of Web Entrepreneurs

Butterfly Women Press
Women Authors Transforming the World

Library of Congress Control Number: 2008929171

ISBN 978-1-932279-96-2

Additional copies of this book are available at www.sherimcconnell.com

Presented by Sheri McConnell Companies, Inc.
24165 IH-10 W, Ste. 217-637
San Antonio, TX 78257 USA
866-821-5829

Editor: Susan Daffron, Logical Expressions, Inc.

Book Design:
Erin Blaskie, Business Services, Etc.
Nancy Cleary, Wyatt-MacKenzie

Butterfly Women Press
an imprint of Wyatt-MacKenzie

www.wymacpublishing.com

Dedicated to all women:
the time is right for you
to own your intuitive power
and bring together *your people*.

Smart Women
Create Membership-Based Businesses

Bonus Chapters

Success and Your Mindset

Who Am I
&
Why I Wrote This Book

My name is Sheri McConnell and I am the president and founder of two national organizations: the National Association of Women Writers (www.NAWW.org) and my second global group, the Association of Web Entrepreneurs (www.AWECONNECT.com).

I also own two high-level information product websites. I teach the membership-based business model at www.createyourgroup.com. I also teach millionaire mindsets and behaviors to women CEOs and entrepreneurs at www.mymillionairegirlfriends.com.

I am one of very few consultants available in the world who can specifically coach individuals on how to create and run a profitable global association, organization, or group of any size from their home!

As the owner of two membership-based businesses, I enjoy a lot of *freedom* in my life. I have the *freedom* to spend more time with my four kids, *freedom* to stay in shape, and *freedom* to earn more than I ever did in the corporate world. In fact, I earn way more than I ever dreamed I could because I own my businesses.

Today I am able to work from my home office in San Antonio, Texas. And the best part is I am able to work with my *ideal customers* on a daily basis, many of whom are six and seven figure earners themselves.

But it wasn't always this way...

When I started my first association back in 2001, I didn't have the **knowledge**, the **skills**, the **money**, or most importantly, the **right mindset about business** to create and run a profitable association. I struggled for more than two years while I learned how to run a profitable membership-based business.

By year three, I had reinvented my first association into a **money-making, revenue-recurring, and passion-fulfilling business**!

In this book, my goal is to teach you to think differently. I want to teach this very powerful business model to you, but most importantly, I want to teach you to think in an entirely new way about how you spend your *life assets*—your time, your money, and your expertise.

Remember, as you take this journey and learn about all the opportunities available to you, don't let negative thoughts creep into your head. Don't think, "This won't work for me." The membership-based business model doesn't fail. YOU are the key to your success.

I speak from experience. I was an only child raised by a mentally ill and very abusive single mom. In my twenties, I married the first abusive man that said I was worthy of love. My point is that if I can heal from my childhood and go on to accomplish more than I ever dreamed possible, all before I turned forty, *so can you.* When you use a proven business model and manage it with the right mindsets, you will achieve more than you ever thought possible too!

To your success,

Sheri

Sheri McConnell Companies, Inc.
National Association of Women Writers
Association of Web Entrepreneurs
Create Your Group
My Millionaire Girlfriends

The Business Model

CHAPTER 1
Building A Virtual Company

CHAPTER 1
Building A Virtual Company

Create Your Own Group

Everything worthwhile in your life only comes into form through your creation. You cannot wait for the right time, the right job, the right husband, the right house, or even the right body to come to you. *You have to create it.* To achieve the life of your dreams, you need to spend time "visioning" what you think will make you happy. Then you get busy "acting," moving forward, and figuring out how to create what you want.

I created the right job by becoming the CEO of my own company and constantly refocusing back to my "passions" during difficult growth phases. And the BIG AHA I had that I want to share with you is that sometimes we go on autopilot. When that happens, we create messes in our lives. Always be willing to scrap some of your creations and start over, whether it's a bad business, bad marriage, or bad eating habits.

Remember, **you have all the power you need within you to create the life you want**.

Why Create A Virtual Group?

When I first started the National Association of Women Writers (NAWW) in 2001, I didn't openly share that I was running and building my new company from my home office. A stigma was attached to having a home office back then; it communicated that you were a small company.

Times have definitely changed.

Fast forward to today. Everything I believed was a weakness in my first business in 2001 is actually a strength that I leverage today to grow my companies.

These are a few reasons why I love virtual businesses. With a virtual business

- You can leverage your low overhead and instead put more money into staff and product and service development.

- You can plug into the latest online technologies to systemize and automate your business.

- You can hire many virtual assistants (VAs) and other online professionals to build and run your business. (Most of us didn't even know VAs existed in 2001!)

- You can easily create a company culture that welcomes creativity, change, and growth.

- You can build equity faster because your upfront investment is incredibly low in comparison to storefront businesses.

- Finally and most importantly, you have no limits to what you can do with a virtual business; you are only limited by your mindsets. (I talk *more about this subject in Chapter Four.*)

Why would you want to build your own membership-based company? Let's discuss a few of the reasons.

Business Equity

I spent a few years working in the corporate world and I can tell you that I certainly didn't have the flexibility I do now. In fact, I even had to sign agreements that the company could use my brilliant ideas whenever they wanted for their profit and that I was not allowed to profit from them.

All wealthy people build equity. They understand that it is smart to work as long as you own what you are working for. When I worked in the corporate world, it was clear that the corporation owned me (mind, body, *and soul*). From my research and experience, I can tell you that most wealthy entrepreneurs build their wealth through real estate and by owning their own businesses.

What is truly exciting is that in the last five years, more and more people are building their wealth by creating virtual online companies for niche target markets they are passionate about.

Life Equity

The bigger reason you should consider building a virtual company *now* is because you are spending your life equity and you can't get it back.

If you are providing a service of any kind, you are trading hours for dollars. You are essentially giving your life away.

If you are a parent like me, the lack of your presence on a daily basis while you trade your life for dollars is having a lasting impact on your children's lives.

In the upcoming chapters, I want to share how you can use the membership-based business model to build a business more quickly than you could build a service-based business, and live a life full of freedom while you do it.

Let's face it, if you can achieve financial independence more quickly than you can in other ways, and leverage your time, expertise, and money exponentially, why wouldn't you?

CHAPTER 2
Start with a Powerful Business Model

CHAPTER 2
Start with a Powerful Business Model

Lots of home-based businesses *aren't "built" to succeed.* Most businesses aren't set up for success. You spend all your time offering services and generating new leads, only to be left exhausted, frustrated, and poor!

Building a membership-based business
(meaning an association or organization or coaching club)
is so much smarter than many other types of business models.

Think about all the service-based solo businesses out there: wedding cake decorators, Web designers, coaches, consultants, professional organizers, copywriters, house cleaners, home decorators, child care providers, and so on.

The amount of money and freedom they have doesn't compare to the lifestyle you can have with a membership-based business!

Here are some comparisons:

- Service-based businesses suck up the owner's time.
- Membership-based businesses let you serve many people at once.

- Service-based businesses only produce income for you when you work.
- Membership-based businesses provide recurring income for years to come even when you aren't working. The money comes in month after month and year after year.

- Service-based businesses can be difficult to distinguish from their competition.
- Membership-based businesses stand out in their chosen niche or industry almost immediately.

- Service-based businesses don't focus on products.
- Membership-based businesses can focus on products that members request. They also have a built-in database of targeted customers.

- Service-based businesses don't provide built-in equity.
- Membership-based businesses naturally let you build equity as you continuously grow the membership.

- Service-based businesses don't provide instant expert status.
- Membership-based businesses naturally position the owner as the go-to person in their chosen field.

Passionate Businesses are More Successful

Being able to connect with like-minded individuals on a daily basis and serve them with my many products and services is very fulfilling.

People tell me I am lucky all the time. Here's why:

- I can take a vacation when I please or take off when I need to when my children get sick.

- I escaped the "cubical farm" and I earn way more than I ever did in the corporate world.

- I am building business and knowledge equity now for all my hard work instead of struggling to move up the corporate ladder (which wasn't easy with children).

- I get to work on products and services I am passionate about.

- I get to spend time with successful individuals I would never be able to meet if I didn't own my associations.

- I am constantly able to invest in myself and increase my knowledge base, so I become even more valuable to my coaching clients and my members.

- I have a flexible schedule. I even completed my Masters in Organizational Management in my free time!

Building A Membership-Based Business
IS SMART...
This type of business has *built in leverage*!

Members renew each year, month, or both! I have many customers that pay for annual memberships, join a monthly coaching program, and sometimes purchase an additional infoproducts all in the same day!

Most importantly, membership-based businesses position you as the gatekeeper to many other successful individuals. *Your database is your golden egg!*

When you are the gatekeeper to many talented people in your niche, *you are* automatically considered an expert! No questions asked. You can also leverage the knowledge and success of your membership too!

When you create and run your own membership-based business, you can:

- **serve customers you are passionate about;**
- **build a business with a strong foundation of recurring customers;**
- **and finally build a business with equity.**

The membership-based business model has attracted some effective free publicity over the years and continues to do so on various levels every single day.

In 2002, just a year after I created the National Association of Women Writers, Writer's Digest named the NAWW website one of the Top Ten Best Websites that year.

I know very well that I didn't have one of the best websites out there at the time. But what I did have was a membership full of writers that might buy subscriptions to Writer's Digest Magazine in the future. The membership-based business model actually encourages large companies in your industry to give you free publicity, even when you are a start-up company. Even when you are small, they assume you are larger than you are because of the business model.

Another example of free publicity that my business model attracted was in 2006 on Christopher Knight's www.ezinearticles.com blog. In case you aren't familiar with this site, he owns the most popular free article site on the Internet.

I have my VAs post all my articles in his database. The links in these articles send my companies an average of 1,000 new visitors a month. One week, I was delighted to find out I was a featured author on his site.

Here is what he said:

> This week's Author Spotlight is on Sheri McConnell, a suggestion from one of our editors that had reviewed her articles. In addition to being an EzineArticles.com Platinum Author, Sheri is also the President of the National Association of Women Writers. When I asked the editor that suggested Sheri for the spotlight this week why she picked Sheri, she said:

> *"Her incoming articles are all approval ready, nothing needing to be fixed or tweaked at all. Also, her articles are very well organized ... they're reader friendly - good voice behind the writing. It's obvious she knows what she's talking about ..."*

> **Looking at Sheri's articles, they appear to have perfect article mechanics:** Good keyword intelligent titles, clean and concise original content as well great

structure from an approving editor's standpoint. The last comment made by the editor was *"I can just scan and approve, especially knowing it's an article of Sheri's."* So the article writing lesson here is that if a little extra time is taken when submitting to make sure the article is "approval ready" chances are the submitted article will be approved much quicker.

Free Publicity Again?

My intuitive powers tell me that I was probably the subject of the blog that day purely because I own a membership-based business. Don't get me wrong, I am grateful any time another company says I am doing a good job, but what I want to make sure you understand is the power of the membership-based model.

I know it is the business model that actually attracts my success because I coach entrepreneurs from various business models. I see very different results even when the marketing strategies are the same. Also, as the founder and president of the National Association of Women Writers (which has more than 3000 women writers now), I see many of these women marketing their books and websites in their service-based businesses day after day. They never garner the type of publicity I receive solely based on the business model I use. That is the main reason I wrote this book and started teaching the six-month coaching programs at www.createyourgroup.com, I wanted to share what I have learned about the membership-based business model from the inside.

These are just a few examples of free publicity. One of the best parts of running a membership-based business has been connecting with other professionals over the years that I had "professional crushes" on. You probably know what I mean. "Professional crushes" are crushes on those mentors and industry leaders or "gurus" you want to connect with but would never have access to with a service-based business.

The membership-based business model has allowed me to connect immediately with professional women I watched on Oprah just hours earlier. I just Googled the name and contacted them. Because I owned a membership-based business, they called me back.

Remember, I created this lifestyle business from scratch as a mother of three back in 2001. I had no experience and no connections. I just had a lot of passion and a willingness to dream and keep moving forward no matter what.

CHAPTER 3
Naming the Network and Serving a Niche

CHAPTER 3
Naming the Network and Serving a Niche

The single most important decision you make when you create a membership-based business is the name of the business.

Choose Your Name Carefully
Your Success Depends On It

The name you choose for your membership-based business is so important that business owners often rename their companies after I start coaching them. Your company name is pure leverage. You can get a lot of mileage out of the name of your company just like I do. What I have learned from working with so many business owners is that your name can really catapult your marketing efforts and accelerate the growth of your new company.

Educating Your Market

I personally love to pick business names that tell exactly what the company does in the name. That way you leverage all you can out of the name when it comes to marketing what you do. You can save yourself so much time and money over the years if you don't have to explain what you do. If you name the company well, the name of your company itself educates potential new customers before you ever have contact with them.

For instance, National Association of Women Writers tells you exactly what we are and the niche we serve. If you don't know we exist, and you sit down at your computer and type "women writers" into Google, you see the National Association of Women Writers is second on the list (as of April 2008).

Your company name is important and affects the success of the company (and the revenues you generate). Other great association names are the Women's Leadership Exchange, National Association of Baby Boomer Women, and the Association of Coaches and Consulting Professionals on the Web. Even if your company isn't membership-based, the name is still important. For example, maybe it is product focused like CreateYourGroup.com. This name tells you exactly what to expect from me.

On the flip side, let's think of a name like Mimeo. What is that? It is actually an online printing company that I love, but the name is hard to remember. I often struggle with spelling it when I am trying to pass along the website address as a resource to my clients. You want to make it easy on your customers to refer you to others. Having an easy-to-remember name is one way to do that.

Global Branding

A *brand* is simply the ideas or images that are connected to a company. In addition to having a name that educates the customer, you should select a name that positions you as a large company from day one, even if you aren't yet. I call this technique "Global Branding." Never create a membership-based business with a regional name. You won't be able to get it off the ground because your reach (the size of the audience or target market that will be interested in your offer) won't be big enough.

After years of working with solo professionals of all kinds, I have discovered that I have a much easier time securing publicity and partnerships based on my name alone. The NAWW sounds big. And we are now, but we weren't in the beginning. People make assumptions based on your company name, so make sure you brand yourself big!

When To Change Your Name

Did you choose your name because it is unique? Or because it has sentimental value? As long as your name tells your target market exactly what you do and makes you sound big, it's okay. If it doesn't, you should seriously consider renaming your company.

CHAPTER 4
Leveraging Your Ownership

CHAPTER 4
Leveraging Your Ownership

When you own a membership-based business, you now have amazing leverage that you did not have as an employee or owner of service-based business.

Many of my clients are amazed that they have this leverage even before they have their first member!

Your ability to understand and use your leverage and the leverage of the group itself is the most critical component to your success. Leveraging accelerates your business growth. Plus, you can leverage more than you might think. You can leverage not only what you have, but also what your partners and members have too. Here are a few examples of leverage.

Leveraging Yourself

- **Your own database.** When you have a member database, other individuals and companies approach you to market their services and products to your membership.

- **Your own knowledge.** People ask you to share your information with their clients, and gain exposure to their databases.

- **Your own success.** Consider the fact that you purchased this book based on the leverage I have because I have two profitable associations.

- **Your time.** I talk *a lot* more about this in the Create Your Group Blueprint and Tool Kit at www.createyourgroup.com. I actually go through six sets of systems that make it possible for you to leverage time in a membership-based business. You learn to leverage your time, so everything you do can attract new customers in three different ways.

- **Your money.** You take the money from your membership-based business (your cash flow) and put it back into the business for additional marketing efforts. You also can apply for business credit before you need it.

Leveraging Others

- **Their database.** In almost every partnership I have, I always request some type of cross-promotion.

- **Their knowledge.** I have been very successful and have made tens of thousands of dollars in extra product sales by leveraging expert speakers in my teleseminars.

- **Their success.** Have your members or partners been on Oprah? Are they well known online and/or offline? You can leverage their popularity.

- **Their time.** Any time you partner with someone successful, spend time with them, or they send a solo e-mail ad on your behalf, you are leveraging the time of others.

- **Their money.** Any time another speaker or partner provides assistance through their virtual assistant or provides exposure in any way to your association (which happens a lot), you are leveraging their money.

Partner With Other Experts Until You Become An Expert Yourself

One of the best strategies I have used to grow my companies was leveraging other people's expertise. As a stay-at-home mom in 2001, I had absolutely no expertise in the publishing/writing industry. I did two things that catapulted my company's success and positioned me as a well-known expert in less than two years.

First, I built my first membership-based business (the National Association of Women Writers). Second, I consistently and systematically leveraged other well-known experts to grow my company.

The key is to leverage the business model. Then you can create a core system to leverage the experts in workshops, conferences, and virtual events.

As you can see, **leverage is one of the main benefits of owning a global group**. In every interview I did with other membership-based business owners, they said the same thing. At www.createyourgroup.com you can see the six different companies I interviewed. Most of them achieved seven figures within five years using the membership-based business model. All of these interviews are included in the Create Your Group Tool Kit in audio CD format and in printed transcript format.

Spend Time Developing Your Unique Expertise

Nothing pays off more than becoming a *unique expert*. A unique expert is someone who has expertise that doesn't already exist and is in high demand. Spend time figuring out what is unique about your expertise. If you don't feel like you have special expertise that is in high demand yet low supply, keep brainstorming and moving forward in your knowledge and experience development until you figure out what you can offer. It may take a while to build a brand around your expertise and position it in a way, so your target market pays a lot for the information you have to share.

Once you develop this expertise and brand yourself in a low-supply, high-demand niche, you are able to leverage your time and money and receive high returns more easily.

For example: I am the only person I know of who is teaching entrepreneurs how to run a national or international membership-based business from home using a virtual team. I niche this information even further by teaching people how to grow their companies to the 6 and 7 figure level in 5 years. I empower many people even further because I do all this while I am raising 4 children.

Because no one is teaching every detail of this business model in the way that I do, I leverage my expertise and sell my $1600 home study program to a target market that values the expertise. Work with a coach to help you develop your expertise. This one strategy is the key to large revenue streams with minimal work.

Let's talk a little more about leverage. **As entrepreneurs all you have to accelerate your growth is your mindset around leverage.**

No matter what business model you use, leverage is important. My favorite way to explain and show you how important leverage is for all entrepreneurs is to discuss **The Leverage Triangle** below.

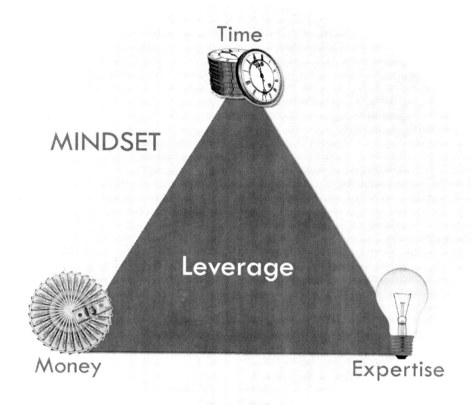

The Leverage Triangle

The Three Elements of The Leverage Triangle

As entrepreneurs and pursuers of our dreams and passions, we all have three elements to work with when we start a business: *time, expertise, and money.*

Most of us have very little of each of these in the beginning of our journey. As we grow our business or our dream of any kind, we begin to have more of each element, and thus more leverage.

Interestingly enough, successful individuals learn to leverage other people's time, expertise, and money too. When we do that, we often help other people reach their dreams. Our dreams are often intertwined. We just don't notice it sometimes.

> *Your mindset determines the amount of success you have and also how fast you achieve it.*

Your mindset determines your success. Period. It is the force and the energy that is driving all those things you need to leverage. The mindset you have is more important than the amount of time you spend on building your dream. It's also more important than your level of expertise, and even more important than how much money you have.

If you aren't operating your passion and dream plan with proven success **mindsets**, you won't be able to leverage your (or anyone else's) money, expertise, and time exponentially.

Leaders Need Support Too

Building wealth is a journey and a way of thinking, and most importantly, a way of acting. If you don't have a support mechanism in place while you are learning the new models and behaviors I talk about in this book, you will probably fail. I hate to be so blunt, but I sincerely have your best interest in mind when I say this. It is the same when you try to work out everyday or achieve any long-term goal. You have to have a support mechanism in place, or you tend to fall back into your old ways. Most people are not taught how to think or act wealthy. Unfortunately, many people I coach get in their own way more than anything else.

How To Manage The Leverage Triangle

Now that you understand The Leverage Triangle and that your mindset is the powerful force driving your ability to leverage time, money, and expertise, certain proven behaviors can help you manage the triangle more productively.

You want to manage the leverage triangle better because managing it more productively helps you reach your dreams more quickly. Here are a few of the behaviors I have all my clients incorporate into their lives:

1. Set boundaries.
2. Hire a team that offers strengths in the areas you are weakest as soon as you can afford them.
3. Focus your energy to eliminate overwhelm.
4. Partner with experts until you become an expert yourself.
5. Package your expertise as a low-supply expertise.

Use Passion As Your Leverage During Start Up If You Don't Have Time, Money, or Expertise

What if you don't have any of the three elements? You don't have time, you don't have money, and you don't have expertise. I do believe you have one last thing to leverage... you can leverage your *passion* to build your dream. *Passion* is an energy force all by itself and when you apply it to a *vision*, you attract the time, money, and expertise you need into your life.

Building Your Dreams and Passion:
The Mindsets To Explore

These are a few of the *mindsets* I encourage you to explore as you build your dreams into a reality, no matter what those dreams may be.

- Understanding your relationship with money itself.

- Looking at the bigger picture, and more importantly, stepping into it.

- Understanding leverage and return on investment (ROI) and using these principles in every area of your life. (*See the ROI questions on next page.*)

- Building a community to serve that you are passionate about.

- Understanding that *you* are the most important resource you have, yet you need a team to accomplish your goals.

- Using technology to build a brand and expert status at lighting speed.

- Plugging into proven (and multiple) business models.

- Surrounding yourself with people who are doers.

- Taking risks and having a sense of adventure and fun.

- Learning about systems and automation, which are the keys to faster success.

- Understanding that you attract specific opportunities when you believe those opportunities are possible.

How To Do A ROI Analysis on Every Area of Your Life

One of the best strategies I share with all my clients is to do a return on investment (ROI) analysis on every decision they make in their lives. Doing an ROI of your time, money, and the sharing of your expertise is crucial when you run a membership-based business. A few questions to consider as you learn to use the ROI mindset are:

- Do I have time to do this?

- Do I have the money to do this?

- Will sharing my expertise in this way benefit my bottom line or bring me new leads?

- Can I leverage this task into other income streams?

- Should I delegate this task?

- Will not delegating this task prevent me from working on more profitable projects?

You should also use the ROI mindset in your personal life. Running a membership-based business from your home office using a global virtual staff means that your business and personal life are meshed together. So it makes perfect sense that to be successful in business, you must look at your ROI at home too. A few questions to consider in this area are:

- Do I have time to take care of these personal duties?

- Can I afford to hire an assistant, housekeeper, or landscaper?

- Can I have someone make prepared meals for my family?

- Can my children ride the bus or car pool with friends to get to and from school?

- Do I have time to volunteer at church or in the community?

Remember to always think about the return on investment of your time, your money, and your energy (mental or physical). Everything you say **yes** to or **no** to has some level of return. You are the only one who can measure the ROI because many of the choices are very personal.

Note: Because your *mindsets are the key* to your success as a woman entrepreneur, I developed a 12-week exclusive program that helps women *learn how to think* in order to successfully build and run a seven-figure virtual business. For more information on the program, visit www.mymillionairegirlfriends.com.

How To Leverage Your Position for Speaking Engagements

Are you a speaker? If you run a membership-based business, the leverage you have to secure speaking opportunities is so much better than most experts or authors who are out there working hard to do the same thing. It isn't fair, but remember, as a president of an association, you have the immediate expert status.

Being the owner of an association where half of the members are professional speakers, I sit in an interesting chair. I see how the ratio of speakers far outweighs the number of speaking opportunities.

I learned that as an association owner, I have a much easier time getting speaking opportunities because again, people want access to my database. It is important to note that when I say that I don't mean that I give them *actual* access; that would be a big 'no-no' and make my members very angry. But with a database, you can let your members know about the conference you are speaking at and encourage them to attend. Many times you are able to easily get a discount for your members.

Another reason you have an easier time getting speaking engagements than most experts, authors, and solo professionals is because you are the President and Founder. This title is really impressive, and people love to have impressive speakers at their conference. Are you starting to understand the leverage you have now?

You Still Have To Be Good

Even though it is easier to get speaking engagements, you still have to be good. Your ability to connect with your target market in person can bring you many clients for years to come. I know this to be true because, for the most part, all the clients who purchase the higher-priced products and services (more than $200) from my associations, I have met in person.

Because I am genuine and really over-deliver in the information I share at conferences, I have built many long-term customer relationships. Many of my customers that attended the first annual NAWW conferences back in 2001 are still NAWW members today. Many of them went on to join the Association of Web Entrepreneurs (AWE) and purchase other related products and services outside of their membership.

If you aren't a professional speaker today, don't worry. You can be when you are ready. Today I love speaking probably more than any other part of the business because I love helping people and connecting with their energy in person.

It wasn't always this way, however. I want to share my struggles with you in the area of being a speaker because I think it is a good example of how bad you can be and still improve. Plus if you are someone who literally experiences physical fear like I did just from the *thought* of speaking, my story may help.

Months before the first NAWW conference in 2003, I repeatedly woke up in the middle of the night thinking about the moment I would be speaking in front of all those people! Fast-forward to today and I can speak in front of thousands of people. All I feel is the passion for the subject I am talking about. It is a very cool feeling!

How did I get my knees to stop knocking? (Literally!)

- **I practiced in front of smaller groups.** In the beginning, I spoke anywhere I could, no matter how small the group. The experience I gained the first couple of years doing that really helped me get better *and more comfortable* at delivering a message.

- **I learned to be prepared.** Knowing the content really helps you not be nervous. When you know the subject matter, speaking also gets easier the more that you do it.

- **I learned how to speak without fear.** I personally struggled with rapid heartbeat, feelings of dread, intense adrenaline rushes, and thought blocking. After learning some physical breathing techniques and learning why my body was doing all this to me, I got much better.

CHAPTER 5
How To Gain Access to CEOs, Authors, Mentors, Coaches, and Business Partners

CHAPTER 5
How To Gain Access to CEOs, Authors, Mentors, Coaches, and Business Partners

In your position as the gatekeeper and owner of a small and eventually large database, you are able to contact and access other high-profile leaders and business owners.

You can partner to create physical and virtual events, and physical and virtual products (ebooks and ereports). You can cross-promote your message across multiple lists, and even share virtual assistants. I always say the Internet is huge, but it is small at the same time. You may be surprised by how many connections your partners have with other individuals you have already worked with.

In my experience, the only challenge you may have in this area is your own mindset. It took me a couple of years before I was comfortable with my role as the leader of an entire association. I quite honestly didn't know what to do with that kind of leverage.

What type of leverage you might ask...

- **Leverage to make more money.** As I mentioned in the last chapter, when you partner, you gain access your partner's database. They also gain access to yours, which paves the way for each of you to get new clients, increase your membership, and make more product/service sales. By access, I don't mean that we give each other actual access to our databases. Rather through the partnership, we cross-promote each other and we gain new subscribers from each other.

- **Leverage to work less.** Naturally, when you partner with someone, you share the work. For instance, you split the work involved in doing a teleseminar, create a product, and so on.

- **Leverage to mastermind.** This type of leverage is my favorite. Two heads are always better than one. Especially when you are talking about two dynamic, highly passionate association or membership-based business owners!

Creating Long-Term Partnerships

Before you even launch your association, put on your leader cap. Start approaching and connecting with those individuals you wouldn't normally be able to access. For instance, having learned about leverage over the last six years at the NAWW, when I launched the AWE in September of 2006, I knew exactly how to leverage the knowledge and prestige of others!

If you visit the AWE at www.aweconnect.com, you will see a list of expert categories on the left-hand side of every page. Most of these experts are 7-figure business owners. With them, I made sure to plan ahead and create win-win partnerships. Each of these experts is an affiliate of mine who earns 50% of sales (my regular affiliate rate is 25%). They also receive exposure on our website through their columns.

In turn, the experts provide content for the website on a monthly basis, a teleseminar on an annual basis, and post announcements in their newsletters regarding membership promotions and events.

In my experience over the last six years of *partnering* with successful and busy business owners, I have learned you should do a few things to ensure a long-term relationship.

1. **Start small.** It makes sense in any new relationship to test the waters. Your partners may have the best intentions to fulfill their obligations, but until you are actually in the trenches, you don't know who or what you are working with. Don't risk too much before you have developed a mutually trusting relationship.

2. **Have fun**. I can't tell you how many e-mails I get where people tell me, "You are so laid back." I guess they expect a president of an association to be stuffy and inaccessible. Connecting with people and being accessible is a major plus. Now, you do have to have boundaries on your accessibility or you will never get anything done. It is a fine balance. For example, I can't stand too much legalese or rules

when it comes to partnerships. I don't mind putting things in writing, of course (which I recommend you do, and you'll find *sample teleseminar speaker agreements in the Create Your Group Tool Kit*). But for me, partners who want to do legal contracts on every single thing we do together are usually too rigid for my style of business.

3. **Select with care**. Make sure you select partners that fit your style of business and your association's culture. When you launch your association, it can start to generate substantial interest anywhere from immediately to six months, depending on the amount of time and money you put towards your marketing efforts. I often tell people that your success is relative to two things: money and time. When you have an association, people want to partner with you, but be selective. When you leverage other people, you also bring along any negative attitudes others might have about them. You, as the leader, have to always be thinking about the perceptions your members/customers have about your partners too. Never be tempted to "gossip." When you partner, you may learn the inner workings of people's businesses. Be professional and don't share the details with other people even if they share their "stuff" with you. I don't gossip in my personal life or in my business life.

4. **Overdeliver**. Always be generous and know that the world is an abundant place. I always try to give a lot more in my partnerships than expected or that is the norm. I love making the partnership offer irresistible.

Remember Your Leverage

As a person who owns a membership-based program, you have the leverage to build partnerships with people that you wouldn't normally be able to approach. Some of these partnerships can turn into profitable and long-term relationships that can literally change your life.

When you are building your membership-based business, one of the best times to approach joint ventures is actually before you launch. Your prospective partners don't expect you to have members yet. They are partnering with you because of the potential your company has long term.

Be A Leader

Running a membership-based company is not always easy. Your members look to you for all the answers *all* the time. However, because you are the leader of a targeted group, you have endless opportunities available to you to encourage positive change in the world.

You not only can encourage change at the grass-roots level, you can have an impact at a broader global level too, thanks to the Internet. You will be approached to do joint ventures, to speak, to partner on projects, to write, to teach, and much more.

Your ability to step into your role as a *leader* determines your rate of success. Notice I didn't say *if* you will be successful. As soon as you learn how to leverage your leadership role, opportunities are just waiting for you. The membership-based business model doesn't fail. Don't be afraid to be a leader today, and create the change you seek in the world.

Make Sure You Invest In Successful Mentors or Coaches

When I started my first company, I looked to other associations for all the answers. But many of them were struggling financially and still are today. So I was essentially modeling strategies that didn't work. I would take advice from anyone, even if they had no experience at what I was trying to accomplish. What often happens in startup is you take free advice because the price is right. Not investing in the right advice is a big mistake. It costs you way more in the long run. Or even worse, you quit before you are able to make the long run.

CHAPTER 6
Building and Managing a Virtual Team

Building and Managing a Virtual Team

Let Go to Grow

Susan Wilson Solovic, author of *The Girl's Guide to Building a Million-Dollar Business* says entrepreneurs have to "*let go to grow.*" This process can require an outside professional to come in and help you manage. You must learn not only how to delegate, but also how to forecast months and years ahead to make sure you will have the cash flow to support the growth. Letting go to grow is liberating. Make sure you view this strategy as an area of continuous learning for yourself. As in any relationship, employee and contractor relationships will take ample amounts of your time to cultivate.

Why I Love Virtual Assistants (VAs)

When I started the NAWW in 2001, I had never heard of a virtual assistant. In case you don't know, a virtual assistant (VA) is a full-fledged small-business owner who works in long-term collaborative partnerships with a small number of regular clients and takes care of all the day-to-day administrative details that prevent a business owner from networking, making calls, giving presentations, creating new products, and so on.

Before I started using virtual assistants in 2004, I tried many other models in my search for help. I tried creating intern and volunteer programs. I even brought in a partner to help. All of these models were time-intensive in the training area. The constant turnover also was a drain on my financial and mental resources.

Before you try to get cheaper help by hiring interns or using volunteers from your own membership, please consider the following:

- VAs are already trained and often even more knowledgeable than you are on the virtual systems you will be using.

- VAs own their own businesses and their livelihood depends on serving you for a long period of time (they want to be part of a team).

- VAs already have their own supplies and invest in their own training (again, they are running a business).

- VAs are considered contractors, and you aren't responsible for all the employee-related costs of having an employee

- VAs network and see the internal workings of their other clients' businesses. They bring this expertise/experience with them to your company.

Weekly Meetings

Having weekly teleconferences with your team is a great practice because it keeps the lines of communication open. As the leader and visionary, this communication also holds you accountable. Nothing is better than a team that wants to keep getting paid to keep *you* moving forward.

My Team

My team meets on Wednesdays. Each member of the team is focused on a specific area such as website building, editing, or transcribing. I also work with each person individually throughout the week by e-mail as needed. Team meetings are great because members on the team need to communicate often to complete projects in a timely matter. It also gives them a time to ask you questions and for you to share your big visions and excitement about what you are doing.

The Main Ingredient of Successful Teams

Leader-driven communication is the main ingredient to building a successful team. Use technology to document start and end dates of projects and use e-mail as much as possible to keep the lines of communication open. One of my VAs uses Basecamp (www.basecamphq.com) to document all the projects she is working on for me. I love it because we formally communicate start and end dates, so I know when to expect projects to be finished. Whatever way you decide to communicate with your team, just make sure you do it on a regular basis. Don't be tempted to save money in this area or think that you should skip a meeting because you are too busy. Lack of communication costs you more money and time in the long run.

Set Up Your Team For Success

As a leader of a membership-based business, it is your job to set up your team for success. You need to let them know what is expected, give them the resources they need, let them know how their work affects others, and reward them when they do a great job. I gave my VAs a bonus last year, and I always try to share knowledge with them in the form of information products or advice on their own businesses. For me, managing a virtual team is organic. I just try to stay real and share my passions. Plus, I always try to let them know how grateful I am to have them with me on my journey!

Prepare For Growth and Hire Before You Need To

Only recently did I see the power of this step in building and managing a virtual team. This mindset is close to the mindset of "the worst time to try to borrow money from the bank is when you need it." Well, the worst time to hire a VA is when you need one.

In fact, I am hiring now for projects and programs I plan to launch later this year. As you grow your membership-based business, make yourself look into the future and plan. Even if you don't have the budget to hire people now, assess your needs and write them down. I can't tell you how many times that I have documented my needs in writing and then later found a way to make it happen, whether it was a person, or a resource. But you have to plan and figure out what you need; otherwise, you won't know what to look for or even notice it when it shows up.

Another Example

This year, I want to add a right-hand person. This person will essentially be another "me," and agree to spend at least 30 to 40 hours a week working on my companies. Obviously this type of virtual assistant can't have many other clients, so my current struggle has been finding a person who can give me that much of her time without it affecting other clients. I think this type of relationship is rare. It takes a special person to care about your business and be passionate about it for around $40 an hour. But I do believe I will find that person. The right person can see the value of being involved in the type of associations I run and be an entrepreneur deep in her heart. I also believe that I will pay quite a lot more than $40 an hour for this person because I want her to be solely focused on my business.

Until you can build your "dream team," you may have to be flexible and add more people to your team that are focused on specific projects. This approach has pluses too because when people are doing more of what they love to do and less of what they *don't* like to do, they are happier.

Slow to Hire; Quick To Fire

As you hire your team members, you can test them. One way to test is to have a probationary period. In this case, you communicate to the person that you have a 90-day probationary period where you both decide if the arrangement is a good fit for each of you. The most common mistake you may make is hiring too quickly and firing too slowly. Remember to trust your gut in this area. If the relationship isn't working, cut your losses and move on.

Where to find VAs

I think the best way to find VAs is to network. Tap into your associations and your professional partnerships. That way, partners and associates can tell you about their experiences with a particular person.

Here is a list of VA Associations you can also try:
• www.assistu.com — AssistU
• www.ivaa.org — International Virtual Assistants Association
• www.canadianva.net — Canadian Virtual Assistant Network
• www.cvac.ca — Canadian Virtual Assistant Connection
• www.multiplestreamsteam.com — Multiple Streams 'Dream' Team
• www.vamatchmaker.com/blog — VA Matchmaker

Other Professionals You Need On Your Team

Besides VAs, you need other professionals on your team. I either have or I am in the process of hiring the following: a new CPA, a marketing consultant or strategist, and a graphic designer.

Outsourcing (The Invisible Team)

I consider the companies I outsource to as members of my virtual team as well. If it weren't for Mimeo.com, I wouldn't have a way to print all my products easily. If it weren't for VistaPrint.com, I wouldn't have a way to print all my marketing materials easily. If it weren't for Lightning Source, I wouldn't have a place to print my books at minimal cost. If it weren't for OfficeDepot.com, I wouldn't have a place to order all my supplies and have them delivered the very next day to my front door.

My virtual outsourcing list goes on and on; you get the idea. All of these companies and their employees are essentially part of your invisible virtual team. By taking advantage of these resources, you can deliver the products and services at minimal cost, so you can have a larger net profit. Before the Internet, we didn't have such easy access to these teams. Today is indeed an excellent time to start a membership-based business.

CHAPTER 7
Having It All Is Possible With Systems

CHAPTER 7
Having It All Is Possible With Systems

In my work with women entrepreneurs, I am often coaching them on how to apply systems to their lives. As a mother of four children and a serial entrepreneur, my use of systems is what makes it possible for me to be able to *do more in less time with less stress*. You can have a family, put them first, and still run a successful business. Don't let anyone tell you that it can't be done. Remember you are the creator of your life. If systems are new to you, it might help to explain what systems are first.

A system is a set of things, actions, ideas, and information that interact with each other and, in so doing, alter other systems. When you start your membership-based business, you create and run a *large system with many smaller systems*. This system is a place of connection for many passionate minds in your chosen niche. In doing so, you alter their systems just like I am here altering yours today. As one of my favorite business writers, Michael Gerber says: "In short, *everything* is a system." In this chapter, I discuss what the high-level systems are in a membership-based business.

For stability and growth, systems are required in all areas of your business. The systems need to be efficient, duplicable, adaptable, and scalable. Systems used repeatedly yield long-term results.

In the Create Your Group Blueprint, I go over all the systems of a membership-based business in detail. In this book, I give you a high-level overview of what they are.

Customer Service Systems

You must make building relationships with your customers the priority in your business, especially when you are running a virtual or online business. Many membership-based, customer-service systems can be implemented and delivered by setting up autoresponders.

Virtual membership-based business customer-service systems let you communicate with your customers in four different areas. You can give feedback, show appreciation, provide education, and send promotions to other members/subscribers.

Time-Management Systems

Improving your time-management systems is a fantastic way to boost your bottom line. If you feel like you have hit a brick wall, focus on these systems. You can see and feel immediate results, so you can move forward. Through automation, delegation, and by getting CLEAR™ (which I discuss on next page) yourself, you can manage your association effectively, profitably, and still have a life full of the freedom you deserve. I also go into detail about the time-management systems I use in the Create Your Group Blueprint.

Here is a high-level overview of the time-management systems I discuss in the Blueprint:
- Online Calendar
- Inbox Organization/Multiple E-Mail Signatures
- Broadcasts/Autoresponders/Digital Delivery
- Automated Recurring Billing

An Overview of Getting CLEAR™

In the bonus section of the Blueprint, I include the complete CLEAR™ program that I developed in 2006 for members of the Association of Web Entrepreneurs. I also talk about it in Chapter 15 of this book. This program integrates the time management and visioning techniques I use to run all four of my companies while raising four children, a husband (Ha!), a weenie dog, and two cats with polar opposite personalities. The point is that if I can do this, so can you! Here is an overview of the program. Even reading through the program at a high level and *acting on it* produces positive results.

Clear the clutter

Clutter takes up physical and mental space. Clutter prevents you from making space for new opportunities. Clear clutter by selecting an area, sorting through it, moving it out, and putting what's left into containers.

Lighten your load

First, take inventory of your responsibilities. Then keep a log of how you spend your time. Be accountable to your schedule and always focus on your top three goals. Cut out everything that doesn't relate to your top three goals.

Establish your goals

Write down your goals and evaluate them against your responsibilities. Goals must be specific, measurable, and realistic. Dream big but give yourself time to implement. Instead of repeatedly doing ready, aim, fire, do ready, aim, fire, fire, fire. It takes time to implement and see results.

Align your goals

Create a timeline. Map out start and end dates. Educate yourself, assemble a team, welcome criticism, and constantly revisit and relearn.

Realize your potential

You are completely responsible for your success. Use leverage to increase your productivity and save time. *Focus* and plan ahead. Take care of your most precious resource—*you*. Do not give yourself, your knowledge, or your time away unless you are completely okay with the consequences of doing so.

Technology Systems

Your success will depend on your ability to embrace and be flexible with technology.

There are only so many hours in the day. Even if you delegate, automation through technology is a lot less expensive in the long run. Here are the technology systems I use to run my membership-based companies. Additional companies are in the resource section of this book as well.

All of the technology systems I use cost me less than $200 in monthly fees. These fees are quite inexpensive considering I run multiple six-figure businesses. You can spend more (you can *always* spend more), but these systems are a great place to start and use as you grow your associations during the first three years. Depending on your growth and advancements in technology, you should always be on the lookout for ways to streamline the processes in your association. Be a geek as much as you can. It literally pays off!

Member Management Systems

One of the main functions in a membership-based business is, of course, managing your members' information. You can manage their data internally or let them do their own updates through your website. Obviously you can save money and time if you let the members do their own updates. Like any technology, probably at least 50 great ways are available that you can use to store your information. Next I describe the information I collect and how I currently manage it.

The System Choices

You probably will have more than one system that you use to manage your member information. At my companies, we are *always* looking for ways to combine our systems. You need at least one system that allows you to do the following with your information:

- Collection and storage
- Printing labels, reports, and directories
- Running reports for strategy planning

The Information You Need to Collect

At your membership-based business, you need to collect the following types of information:

Contact Information
Information such as the member's name, address, phone number, and e-mail address can be stored virtually at Practice Pay Solutions. You can then download the data into a database on your hard drive. At NAWW, I use this information as a tangible benefit by turning it into the member directories that go out in the membership boxes.

Payment Information
Credit card information and expiration dates can also be downloaded from Practice Pay Solutions to QuickBooks for storage on your hard drive.

Interests

You should capture other information such as such as the member's website address. At the NAWW, we also categorize published and non-published authors. This information is collected in fields we created in our My Mail List database that resides on our hard drive.

Purchased Products and/or Services

Knowing exactly what your clients purchase is the most valuable information you can collect and analyze. Running reports on this information in your database and/or in QuickBooks lets you plan ahead because you can budget accordingly based on projected revenues for similar products and services you add later. You also can run reports and target customers based on their previous purchases with various marketing campaigns. For instance, I always make sure that customers who attend virtual and/or live events are notified about similar upcoming events.

Prospects

On my hard drive, I also have a record of each person who has ever contacted us to request information. Many people will not join after you mail them a brochure. Make sure you collect people's mailing information so you can mail out postcard promotions in the future. Personally, I focus on online marketing because it is less expensive and the ROI is so much higher. But postcards do work well to advertise regional smaller events.

Other Programs (Coaching and Workshops)

Once you start creating multiple streams of income within your membership-based business, you should create a field in your database or a checkbox that lets you quickly run a report to find out who is in a certain program.

Strategy Planning and Your Reports

As I mentioned, you can run reports with the information that you have in your database. I currently use My Mail List for all the member information storage (other than financial). Remember that your database is only as good as the information that is stored in it. The more information you add to it or have your members enter in, the more you can use it for strategic planning. From My Mail List, I can pull reports on the following information:

- Renewal Dates. I send out renewal postcards by filtering by the current month in the database.

- Products and Services. I filter previous purchases to target past customers for new products and services.

- Cities and States. I filter this information for our printed directories at the NAWW and to see where all of our members are concentrated so we can plan physical events.

- Type of Members. I filter published and non-published members; I also filter coaching clients from non-coaching clients.

- Websites. I search for keywords in a URL if my team or one of the members requests a certain resource.

- Referrals. I also note who referred the member if they specified a company or person or Regional Representative. For example, many members join the NAWW from our print ad campaigns at *Writer's Digest*. We also run reports to track that we are consistently getting enough members to justify the $8,000 a year we spend on those ads. Our online affiliate program also tracks this type of information automatically for the online affiliates.

Promotional and Lead Generation Systems

Your Website's Sole Purpose: Collecting Customer Information in Exchange for a Freebie

On every page of your website you *must* offer one or more of the following: a free ezine, a free ereport, a free audio class, or free access to a teleseminar. Because 99% of the people that visit your website will not purchase anything on the first visit, it is *crucial* that you build a relationship with them. You can't do this if you can't contact them.

Marketing Funnels

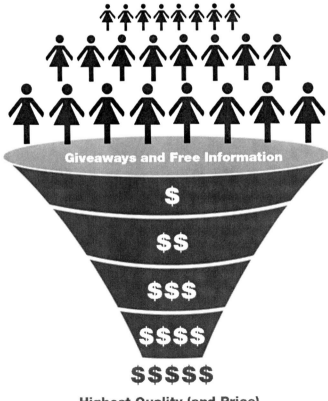

**Highest Quality (and Price)
Products & Services**

Remember that your *ideal targeted prospects* are most often going to enter your marketing funnel by requesting a freebie from your website. I say "most often" because you should also collect information offline at events too. Then have an assistant enter the email addresses into your website sign-up box.

Understanding the Funnel

Your prospects move down the funnel as they join your association and/or purchase other products and services. As they move down the funnel, you continuously build a trusting relationship by delivering high-quality products and services at different price points that help them with their problems. The prices of the products and services increase as your customers move down the funnel.

Keep an Open Door

If you look at the funnel picture on the previous page, you can visually see how your prospects enter your funnel. Of course, you don't want your customers to leave your funnel, but sometimes they will. I have found with membership-based businesses as long as you keep an open door, many of your customers eventually come back. Many members may not renew for a couple of years, but then renew when they need your products or services again. Some people may receive your free newsletter for years and never join as a member, *but* they will purchase a lot of your products and services instead.

Using the FOCUS Marketing Method To Stay On Track

In the Blueprint and Tool Kit, along with the Get CLEAR™ program, I also include my FOCUS Marketing Method™ in detail. If you purchase the Blueprint, I encourage you to post the Mind maps from both of these programs in your office as reminders to help you stay motivated. Here is a high-level overview of the FOCUS Marketing Method™:

Filtered. All of your marketing copy should focus on your ideal niche so you are filtering your members. You only want to serve those you love working with and have passion for.

Organized. Your marketing plan needs to be organized. Map out your annual sales, new launches, and schedule ongoing follow-up.

Converts. Your goal is to convert prospects into customers. Follow this process flow for converting customers: Add New Subscribers… Build Relationships… Turn Into Members and Customers … Turn Into Loyal Recurring Members and Customers.

Utilize. Use current marketing theories that already exist, such as SWOT Analysis, Marketing Funnel, and the P's of Marketing.

Systematic. Use automation and the natural selling cycles (closing, resell, and upsell).

Product & Service Development Systems

As the owner of a membership-based business for your industry, you can develop solutions in the form of information products and other online educational services such as virtual learning events and teleseminars/webinars.

Creating Infoproducts

You can use information products (or "infoproducts") in your membership-based business in a number of ways.

My system includes:
- Giving a free report to new subscribers to educate them about the membership-based business and build a relationship.

- Sending an information product as a follow-up to potential members you meet while networking.

- Selling infoproducts as standalone products on a website and at events

- Wrapping a product into the membership benefit package

- Giving products to strategic partners as bonuses

Where To Find Content

Look around for content you already have. Many professionals (like you) have a lot of content available on their hard drives.

Take inventory and see what you have.

Do you have any of the following?

- Handouts from your previous speaking events.
- PowerPoint presentations from your previous speaking events.
- Project notes.
- A group of articles you've written for a targeted audience.
- Audios of your speaking events.
- A list of resources for a targeted audience.
- A group of contacts that you compiled for a certain market.

More on Infoproduct Development and Launch

On the following pages, I have included two high-level visual overviews of the infoproduct creation cycle and the infoproduct launch cycle I use at all four of my companies. Publishing information products within and outside of your membership packages is also a profitable business model to pursue.

Information Product Creation Cycle

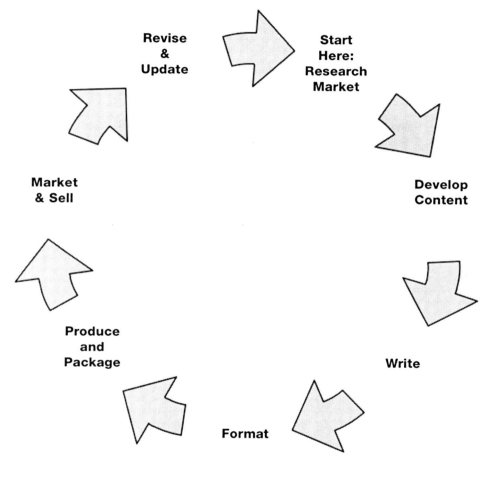

Information Product Prelaunch Cycle

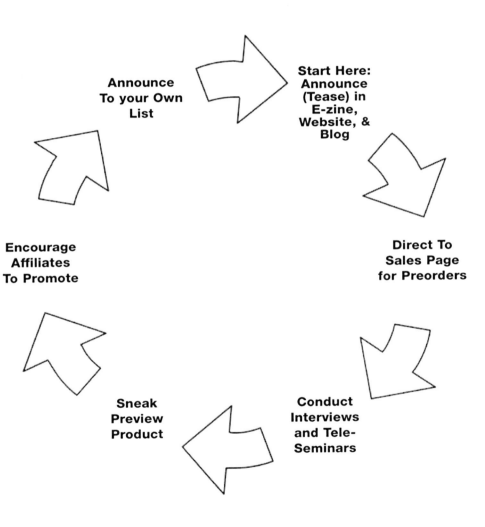

Announce To your Own List

Start Here: Announce (Tease) in E-zine, Website, & Blog

Encourage Affiliates To Promote

Direct To Sales Page for Preorders

Sneak Preview Product

Conduct Interviews and Tele-Seminars

CHAPTER 8
The Changing Face of Virtual Networks

CHAPTER 8
The Changing Face of Virtual Networks

Big Companies Vs. Small Companies

In the virtual world, the size of the company does not always reflect the size of the bottom line. Online, companies' bottom lines often grow into the millions (yes, millions) with a few employees and a dozen or so virtual staff.

The old brick and mortar association with the large board of directors is a thing of the past. Today's virtual membership-based business CEO makes decisions and implements at lightning speeds compared to just a decade ago. Over the last five years, owners of bricks and mortar membership-based businesses are also learning to use the power of the Internet because they experienced quite a drop in renewals as the Internet allowed more Internet-savvy groups to compete for their members.

Because of the Internet, **you can achieve more with less effort.** You can network faster and with more people online through social networks like Facebook and Linked In.

Because of the Internet, **you can give your customers more value while incurring less expense**. You can teach them through online teleseminars, webinars, or with information products like ereports and ebooks for pennies.

Because of the Internet, **you can implement everything in less time**. This applies to marketing campaigns, website launches, and joint venturing. In the old days, it took weeks to get print marketing into your customer's hands. Now, you can connect with customer in minutes using your own database of subscribers.

A few pieces of advice if the membership-based business is your first business:

Use Passion As Your Leverage During Start Up

I have already talked about leverage and the three elements you have to leverage in start up. You can leverage money, time, and expertise. I also told you that your mindset is the force that leverages these three things. Most of the time, when you begin to build wealth you will have at least one of these three things and that is what you use for your beginning leverage.

Like I said before, if you don't have any of the three elements you can leverage your *passion* to build your dream. *Passion* is an energy force all by itself, and when you apply it to a *vision*, you attract the time, money, and expertise you need into your life.

Develop Your Business Intuition

When you develop your business intuition, you don't have to look to others to give you strength or to teach you what they know. Using your business intuition, you can look internally, find the answers and the strength to be bold, and act on your inner guidance. Proactively accessing your intuition requires you to listen and pay attention to these mental insights. Your insights help you keep moving forward. The more you trust these insights, the more your craft or expertise improves. Of course, you must add liberal amounts of perseverance and some organizational skills as well, but the end results pay off as you see your dreams and goals come to fruition.

Your Lifestyle Has To Drive The Company

As the CEO of your membership-based business, it is helpful to do what I call "Practice Conscious Living." People who achieve their dreams do it with a plan. They may start out simply doing something they are passionate about, but eventually to achieve substantial results, they had to sit down and map out a plan. People who achieve dreams make changes in their lives and live in a very conscious way. They pay attention to what they have said yes and no to, and choose how they react to negative people and situations. They also consciously choose to surround themselves with other people who have had fun accomplishing their dreams. People who achieve their dreams are disciplined about their choices and chose to consciously enjoy every moment they can going forward.

From this day forward, I encourage you to begin to practice conscious living. Make sure you aren't on autopilot. How do you know if you are on autopilot? Sometimes making excuses or blaming others can be a sign that you are living your life on autopilot. Often situations in our lives or behaviors we have learned in childhood can be the reason we don't know how to live life in a conscious way. One of my favorite phrases is "You do better when you know better." Don't look back; just look forward. And don't wait another day to get busy living life in a way that feels joyful to you.

Rome Wasn't Built In A Day

It takes at least a year to build strong customer relationships, which are the foundation of your business. After a while you begin to experience a momentum of repeat customer purchases. Virtual membership-based businesses naturally lend themselves to word of mouth referrals. And if what you built isn't something that is fun to run anymore, rebuild it! I totally reinvented the NAWW at the end of the second year to be the association I really wanted to run. I stopped doing annual conferences and went completely virtual instead. It was a more profitable decision for my companies and a lot more fun to manage too.

CHAPTER 9
The 6 Keys To Creating a Highly Profitable Membership-Based Business

CHAPTER 9
The 6 Keys To Creating a Highly Profitable Membership-Based Business

After seven years of running online membership-based companies, I have come up with six important keys to keep the cash flow "flowing" in.

They are:

Key One

You must offer tangible items that your target market will pay for month after month and year after year.

Key Two

You must choose your name carefully using my two criteria which are keywords and global branding.

Key Three

You must build a leverageable brand for members and representatives to plug into.

Key Four

You must focus on the bottom line and always do an ROI analysis on your time, money, and expertise. Do this in the business and in your life.

Key Five

You must understand how to leverage your role as the gatekeeper and president and founder of your membership-based business.

Key Six

You must look at everything as a system that you or your team can create or improve.

Bonus Chapters
Success and Your Mindset

Chapter 10
Lifestyle Tips for Women Who Think & Create Big

Chapter 10
Lifestyle Tips for Women Who Think & Create Big

Much of my success with membership-based businesses is also because of my ability to continuously grow in the area of "mindsets". Here are a number of tips to help you *think and create in a big way*.

Tip One

Honor Your Urges

One of the main reasons I left the corporate world and took the entrepreneurial plunge many years ago was so I could do more of what I enjoyed and less of what I hated. It makes sense doesn't it? Yet, you would be surprised how many entrepreneurs don't do more of what they love. Make sure you take advantage of the freedom you have by setting boundaries early on in your business. Successful entrepreneurs don't create boundaries after they are wealthy. They create them so they can become wealthy. Not always being accessible actually creates scarcity and attracts more business. From now on when you want to take off and head to Starbucks or you want to take a week off and go on vacation, honor those urges, plan accordingly, and then do it.

Tip Two

You Can Work Hard and Still Have Fun

When you first start your company, you probably will wear all the hats and work harder than you ever have. But once the business is built and you start to gain new customers and sell products, it is a lot of fun. The best part of being a leader is being able to pick up the phone and have access to someone you have admired for years because you are a gatekeeper to a database of customers. You learn so much from those experts you now have access to, and your customers will love you for it when you graciously pass new information on to them.

Tip Three

Hit the Gym

Look around at the most successful people and what do you see. You see individuals that invest in their bodies as much as they invest in their businesses. How you feel, how you look, and your vitality in general are all-important factors in creating your wealth/life plan.

Tip Four

Pay Attention to Your Surroundings

Your environment contributes to your overall success in many ways. Just like certain types of fish, your business and personal growth will come to a complete halt based on the size of your "tank," As an entrepreneur, you should consider not only the size, but also many other elements of your *think tank*.

1) The size of the space. Do you have enough space to hold meetings with clients or to process packages? Can you spread out when you need to work on a large project? Does your chair bump into the wall?

2) The lighting. Do you have adequate lighting? Can you relocate your home office to a room with lots of windows?

3) The strategies in place to keep you organized. You must have a system in place to manage all the people, ideas, and projects you encounter as you grow your company. Visit www.elizabethhagen.com for excellent help in this area.

4) The tools you need to do your job. Is your office equipment functioning properly? Have you invested time in learning how to manage important tools that run your business?

5) The boundaries you have set. How do you manage interruptions? How do you manage e-mail? If you don't have a system in place with specific time management rules, your bottom line will suffer. Timothy Ferriss's *4 Hour Work Week* is an excellent resource on this topic.

6) The overall energy of the space. Is your furniture old? Is the space clean and inviting? Does the color affect your mood in a positive way?

Tip Five

Let Go & Have Fun

One of the main reasons I became an entrepreneur and left the corporate world back in 1999 was because I loved the freedom to just let go and have fun. I wanted to have a higher quality of life where I could be creative and earn more for that creativity. Unfortunately, what happens with many entrepreneurs in start up is they get too intense and end up chasing away the most beneficial business and personal relationships. Always remember "why" you are pursuing this dream in the first place and remember to let go and have fun with the people you meet and do business with. I *love* working with people who make me laugh, who have a wicked sense of humor, who get passionate about their causes, and who know how to let go, be themselves, and make "work" fun. The cool thing is these types of people attract others like them, and your fun "network" then multiplies exponentially. So do your revenues. Bottom line: Letting go and having fun in business is good for the soul and for the bank account.

Tip Six

Build Millionaire Relationships

NO ONE can reach seven figures without building crucial business and personal relationships along the way. The membership-based business model is a millionaire business model and by using it, you attract important relationships more easily. Millionaire relationships aren't always measured by the financial return on investment (ROI) you receive either. One of the most exciting parts of building a company that you are passionate about is all of the dynamic and energetic people you can access. This type of ROI often shows up in the form of real people who serve as resources when you need them. All you have to do is decide to take *action* and work on getting to know people. Then you can communicate how your company can help them solve their problems.

Tip Seven

Understand Entrepreneurial Energy

Millionaires rarely sit down, and they are often in great shape. They also don't watch TV much, and they give of themselves freely. Millionaires have lots of entrepreneurial energy. They are creative, passionate, risk takers, who are big thinkers and always evolving. If this description isn't you yet, start aiming for these behaviors today. Know that what you eat and *if* you exercise directly affects your bottom line. People are attracted to people (and companies) who take care of themselves and are full of energy. What you feed your brain (literally) determines your ability to solve million-dollar problems and come up with million-dollar ideas. (Just some food for thought!)

CHAPTER 11
How to Create Passionate Connections

CHAPTER 11
How to Create Passionate Connections

Do you feel validated? I heard Oprah once say that she thinks everyone on this earth has one basic need: to be validated. I know when I started the National Association of Women Writers, it was because I needed to find other women who loved to write and create like I do. I needed to learn with them and laugh with them because I yearned for the validation that I would receive. In turn, I validated those writers too. Little did I realize at the time how many women all over the world needed their goals and dreams affirmed just as I did.

I too believe that validation (or "passionate connections" as I like to call them) is important. In fact, I think it's so important I have built multiple companies with that vision in mind. Here are a five ways I have learned to create passionate connections and validate others over the last seven years as I grew the NAWW and my other companies. No matter what your goals are, I know you can meet them by reaching out to validate others and following the tips below. Enjoy the journey!

Be of Service

Do you know what Web 2.0 is? It is the evolution of the current state of the Internet. Web 2.0 includes the trend of social networking and all of the technology that supports it. I love that the present culture of the Internet has evolved to focus on people and that Web 2.0 technology makes it easier to be of service. Being of service and helping others feel good about themselves is not only rewarding, it helps you grow exponentially. You grow internally as a person and externally because your influence has a farther reach.

Be a Problem Solver

When you focus on helping people with their problems in your writing and in your products/services, you build a strong foundation of support for yourself. Always connect by sharing a part of your personal life, but remember that creating passionate connections with others by solving their problems should be the focus in all that you do. I always tell my kids, "solve problems; don't create them!"

Be Not Afraid

The only way I know to accomplish big dreams is to take risks and move through fear. You know the dreams I am talking about. The ones we had when we were young, before we gave up and decided to be "practical." Don't be afraid of fear and the muddled mind feeling. As you reach out and help others, you will receive the resources you need. Take the risks you need by basking in that uncomfortable feeling of trying something completely new. Taking risks is even harder if it isn't something you do often. I now do it so often that taking risks seems a normal part of my day.

Be a Visionary

Use your creativity to craft life visions for yourself and others. Most people don't spend any time at all on visioning what they want in their lives. Visioning is the key to making long-lasting passionate connections with everyone you come in contact with. Be a dreamer and then follow through with action. Trust me; this simple tip attracts like-minded individuals into your life. Together you can achieve more than you ever could alone. Don't worry if you get overwhelmed. Being a visionary is supposed to be overwhelming to some extent. But visioning works on many different levels too. Try breaking it down by creating smaller visions for your family, your significant other, your work and/or business goals, and so on.

Be Real

This tip is my favorite one for creating passionate connections because it helps others the most. Think about all the times someone was honest with you and it pushed you forward. When someone cared enough to validate you by showing you that you were worth the time to talk, laugh, and learn with. Remember when you were a kid. Isn't that all you wanted back then? Relationships that were real and honest. Be real with those you come in contact with (whether personal or professional), and you will create a life-long stream of validated friends and/or customers to serve.

What it all boils down to is that life is about making passionate connections. It is about validating others and allowing them to live dreams that touch other people's lives too. When your dreams include serving others, you can't lose. Make sure you practice the tips, so you are doing your part to make an incredible life happen for you.

CHAPTER 12
How To Tap Into Your Brilliance (For Writers)

CHAPTER 12
How To Tap Into Your Brilliance (For Writers)

As a practicing writer, do you sometimes feel like you have nothing to write or like it takes forever to create even one well-written sentence? And after all the hard work it took to create a powerful sentence, article, or book, then you struggle to get motivated to do it all over again. Writing doesn't have to be this difficult. You can learn to **tap into your brilliance** easier, faster, and with more excitement!

Creating A Supportive Environment

Writing partners are a must. More than anything else, a writing buddy or partner allows you to be validated on a consistent basis. Not just validation of your actual writing, but validation of your time and work. That is why joining organizations like the National Association of Women Writers (NAWW) is so important in helping you tap into your brilliance. It really is about validation of your purpose. You won't sit down at the computer again and again to write if you don't feel like it is a worthwhile experience.

Organization isn't just for people who are anal. When you are organized, your mind can tap into ideas and thoughts more quickly. If you have a disorganized life, your brain often resembles the same disorganized state. A clogged faucet doesn't flow.

Interviews are another great way to allow yourself to tap into your own brilliance. Whenever I am stuck with a writing project, I schedule an interview to help me get stimulated again. First, it gives me the accountability to get questions created for the interviewee, and second, I am always energized by the "brilliance" of other dynamic people. I get new ideas and inspiration each and every time I do an interview. Plus I get great quotes I can infuse into my own writing.

Practicing Organic Writing

Look for the seeds. These are the starter ideas that you usually get throughout your days. I get lots of them in the shower. When you sit down to write, start writing about what you are most passionate about first. Make a list of bullets first, and expand upon those for additional ideas. Write often and you will train yourself to "get in the flow" more easily.

A few other great ways to "grow" your ideas into other writing projects organically is to take inventory of what you already have. Use past content to jumpstart your writing. Pull quotes from books you love and have read over and over again.

Using the Right Tapping Tools

Some people like to generate ideas and tap into their brilliance in a linear way with tools such as outlines. Other people prefer using a more visual and creative approach, such as mind mapping. I use both. When I work on any project that has a table of contents, I always start with it first. I know that my table of contents won't look the same in the end. But having it as a starting point gets me going. I also create "dummy" covers and slide them into a 3-ring binder with the table of contents right inside in front of a lot of blank hole-punched paper. I carry this binder around and jot down new ideas and stick notes in the pockets.

When I write shorter articles, I use mind maps to map out the flow of the information. I also love using mind maps to plan and write work-shops or teleseminars because the mind maps become an extra visual bonus for the attendees. I use a program called Mind Manager Pro from Mindjet Software (www.mindjet.com) for this purpose.

You can also use a dry-erase board and sticky Post It notes that you can move around to organize your ideas. On the days when I can't write at all, which for me is usually the weekends, I also put ideas on sticky notes and stick them to my computer. This one practice alone allows me to easily tap right into my brilliance when I sit back down at the computer on Monday morning.

Focusing on the Rewards

Focusing on rewards is an effective way that I have trained myself to tap into my brilliance. I set deadlines and reward myself with time off to read a book and grab some Starbucks coffee. I also announce my accomplishments to my internal team and support group. I also offer preorders for products I haven't yet written to my customers. That financial reward alone (much like a book advance) completely moti-vates me to tap into my brilliance because I know I can't disappoint my customers.

Invitation to Tap Into Your Brilliance

When you let go of perfection and create the right environment to sup-port your dreams and passions, you can tap into your brilliance more easily. The systems I talk about in this book help you train your brain to work faster and more easily. If you need additional support as a writer, visit NAWW at www.naww.org.

CHAPTER 13
Creating Your Healthy Money Mindset

CHAPTER 13
Creating Your Healthy Money Mindset

Your money mindset affects your ability to dream big and live your life's passion in three ways.

#1

Believing in Abundance

Right now you believe many goals are attainable and many are not. The way you were raised and your current environment dictate your beliefs. Unless you are challenged and taught to believe differently, you stay stuck. Today, open up your mind to abundance. Take a financial goal and write it down with an abundance mindset. Try to make yourself believe that you can meet the goal even if a nagging voice in your head is saying "no way!" Then put the piece of paper where you can see it every day. Write down whatever you want to do or have. It doesn't matter. Think abundantly and think big for yourself.

#2

Manifesting What You Want

Once you begin to think more abundantly and do it enough that it becomes a practiced mindset, you begin to easily manifest what you need, want, and deserve in life. Since manifesting is done in the mind, it in itself, is another mindset. You should begin to consciously manifest what you dream of and what you need to accomplish your dreams. That is why writing down your financial goals is so powerful. It forces you to consciously manifest your wants and desires.

Welcoming the Change

The third mindset, and the hardest and most important, is being open to change. Many of us are very fearful of change and don't recognize that we are resisting an abundant life because of the safe choices we make.

Creating Your *Dreams and Passion* Bank Account

Nothing creates accountability and forces you to dream more than owning a company that you are passionate about. **We all have dreams and passions that are also profitable entrepreneurial ventures.** Most of us just don't take the time to do the work to search our souls and figure out what profitable passions are inside of us. Sad, isn't it?

Loral Langemeier refers to it as creating your cash machine: your capacity to create revenue to fuel your wealth and live your dreams. Timothy Ferriss calls it Dreamlining; simply put, these are timelines of your dreams and how much money you will need to realize those dreams. Read more about Dreamlining here and get a six-month timeline at:

http://www.fourhourworkweek.com/ferriss-resources-lifestyle.htm

When I am coaching, I always have my clients start by filling out "passion worksheets" if they don't know what they want to do. It is easy to become overwhelmed with the thought of picking one passion to pour your heart and soul into. But I know that if you create a business from your dreams, the universe rewards you for honoring yourself and begins to send money your way. This money helps you further fuel you dreams and passion bank account.

Growing and Funding Your Dreams and Passions

I really want you to begin to understand how to use financial goals to motivate you to dream bigger and to act within a time frame.

It is an amazing feeling to be able to grow and fund your dreams and passions and teach others to do the same. It feels even better when you can fund charities that you care about.

To grow and fund your dreams and passions, you must invest in knowledge. Just as I discussed earlier, most of us aren't brought up with healthy money mindsets. To grow and fund your dreams and passions, you must invest in the knowledge that will help you learn the following:

- How to earn money with your passions.

- How to keep as much money as possible after you earn it.

- How to manage and grow a team (preferably a virtual team).

- How to communicate your dreams and passions to your team.

- How to make decisions that do not undermine your overall dreams.

- How to continue the cycle of dream growth by mentoring others.

- Be willing to spend a significant percentage of your time learning from others, and seek the right team members to help you grow and fund your dreams and passions. Learning takes time and money, but the reward is exponentially greater than the cost.

Living Your Dreams

I want to wrap up by reminding you to constantly revisit your *dreams and passions* by journaling and asking the most important question of all: why?

Every person who *lives his or her dreams* eventually becomes muddled in the day-to-day business stuff that has to be done in order for our dreams to blossom. When you get to a point that you are feeling an energy drain from living your dreams instead of an energy surge, it is time to ask yourself why you started living this dream in the first place.

By focusing on that initial reason that you began the dream, you really pinpoint the place in time when you were in a creative flow and more fulfilled. It may be time to change and grow and move on and live a new dream or it may be time to eliminate some energy drains that wiggled their way into your life when you were too busy to notice.

Just make sure you slow down often so you can focus on the process of living your dreams while you are in the middle of living them. After all, that is what it is all about!

CHAPTER 14
How To Stay Motivated

CHAPTER 14
How To Stay Motivated

When you run a membership-based business, it's a lot of work, and sometimes it's hard to stay motivated. Here is how I have rejuvenated myself over the years.

Find a Natural Sanctuary

Stimulate the Senses

One of the best ways to stay motivated and to sustain your passion (no matter what it is) is to get outside and walk, jog, or run. Our bodies and our brains need to be stimulated and nothing does this better than nature. Nature is vivid. The sounds and textures and smells help you come alive. By physically moving in nature, you stimulate your body even more. Once your senses become stimulated, your brain starts to give you answers to personal and/or business questions. Your body also becomes programmed to generate new creative ideas when you stimulate your senses.

Clearing the Clutter and Chaos

One reason we lose our motivation and can't find our passion in life is that we are too busy experiencing chaos. Chaos comes in many forms. It can be in the form of people, events, TV, radio, and so on. You must experience nature to find and sustain your passion. Spending just 30 minutes a day outside clears the clutter from your brain and reprograms you to breathe and think more instead of reacting to all the numbing stimulants in your life!

Create a Fun System

Journaling

Once you clear your mind each day, you will need a *fun* system to keep track of all the stimulating ideas you get! I have a notebook that I carry with me where I jot down affirmations, goals, and problems (personal and professional) that I need to solve. I find that every few months or so I like to rip it all out, throw it away, and start over. For me, after I solve all those problems and reach all those goals, I like to physically start over with a clean slate and move on. Be open to the process of journaling and do what your gut tells you to do.

Mind Mapping

I also love mind mapping because I am drawn to the creative visuals! Some great resources are available like the software from Mindjet (www.mindjet.com) that I mentioned before. For me, the process of mind mapping stimulates the creative side of my brain.

Visioning

The other fun way I stay motivated and connected to my passion is by using a graphic coach. My coach, Christina Merkley at www.shift-it-coach.com took me through her Shift It Program. Not only was this fun, it was eye opening! She also has maps and instructions so you can use this graphic coaching process yourself at home.

Pay Attention

The wonderful thing about creating a fun system in your daily life and getting back to nature is that it gives you the time and space to "ask yourself questions." This step is the key to sustaining your passion. Over time, you change, and the world around you keeps changing too. It is important (now more than ever) that you keep asking yourself questions so you can stay centered. What types of questions should you ask yourself in order to sustain your passion?

What makes me happy?

What do I enjoy?

What excites me?

What makes me cry?

What can I do to learn more about my passions?

How can I use my passion to improve the world around me?

Am I doing anything creative in my life?

If not, what can I do?

Make sure to revisit these questions often. I use a visioning journal. Again, make sure to check out the tools I use often to manifest my passions more clearly at www.shift-it-coach.com.

CHAPTER 15
Get CLEAR About Success

CHAPTER 15
Get CLEAR About Success

Have you been struggling to reach your goals and achieve the level of success you desire and deserve?

Then use tips from my CLEAR™ Program on the following pages to get the results you want.

CLEAR™ Program

Clear the Clutter

The first step in the process is to eliminate the clutter that takes up physical and mental space in your life. Your goal is to make room for your future by getting rid of the excess "stuff" that creates chaos in your surroundings and clogs your mind with overwhelm.

To clear the clutter, first you need to select an area to work on, whether it is your desk, your home office, or some other space that's in disarray. Then implement a sorting strategy to 1) throw away things you don't use or need; 2) give away or recycle items that someone else can use; and 3) put items in their place. Put paperwork and other documents you need in file folders, and place your tools of the trade and other supplies in containers. Everything should have its own designated space so you can find things quickly and easily every time you need them.

Clearing the clutter frees up your mind to focus on matters that are important to you. You'll be amazed at how much more time and energy you have to do the things you love and that bring you the highest return when you've purged your physical space and put systems in place to keep you organized for the long term.

*L*ighten Your Load

This next step involves taking inventory of your responsibilities, and deciding which priorities are most important to help you meet your goals. Then you must either delegate those things that can be done by others so you're not trying to do everything yourself, or say "no" to projects and obligations that prevent you from achieving your objectives.

Managing your time is key because it's easy to sabotage yourself by taking on too much. Pick your top three priorities. Then set boundaries so you can stay focused and on track. Use a time-blocking strategy to plot your scheduled tasks and stick to your schedule as much as possible. Treat yourself as if you were a client. You must get the work done, so focus on doing just that.

Another time-management strategy is to build accountability into your system. Enlist a buddy or a team member to hold you responsible for achieving the goals you've set for yourself. Also make sure that others don't overstep their bounds by expecting you to do things that are not in alignment with your priorities. Learn how to say "no."

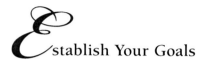stablish Your Goals

Your ultimate success relies on having, and reaching, a concrete set of goals. Using your top three priorities from the "Lighten Your Load" section as a guide, put your goals in writing and evaluate them against your responsibilities. Ask yourself: Are my goals specific? Are they measurable? Are they realistic?

You need to be very clear and concise about the outcomes you want to achieve, and the timelines that are involved in getting from one milestone to the next. This clarity helps guide you to accomplish tasks, measure your progress, and be accountable for your time. It also helps ensure that your goals are in alignment with the rest of your life. If you aren't clear about your outcomes, you will continue to struggle with frustration and overwhelm as you try to find balance.

Align Your Goals

As you're establishing your goals and setting timelines, you must evaluate your current responsibilities against your goals. You will probably discover that you have to include other activities in your timeframe too, such as taking classes, creating joint venture partnerships, outsourcing projects, and building a team of people who can help you get from where you are to where you want to be. These activities are part of aligning your goals to make sure they fit with your life. Having a team and asking for their input also helps you learn what is and isn't working so you can make necessary changes and improvements in your systems and products.

Every year, you should revisit and realign your goals so you're keeping up with industry trends and technological advances that can help you maximize your time and run your business more efficiently. When you do, you align yourself for success.

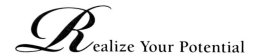

ealize Your Potential

Realizing your potential is the result of all the work you've done so far. You've cleared the clutter, lightened your load, established and aligned your goals, so you are responsible for your own success. Now you can use leverage to realize your potential. You can leverage your time to increase productivity; leverage other people's time and energy to do the tasks you delegate to them; create partnerships with others so you can leverage their contacts and database to expand your market reach; and leverage your knowledge to create information products that are out there selling for you even when you're not working.

As the owner of a membership-based business, you are now focused with accountability built into your system to keep you on track, and you're delegating, outsourcing, and using leverage to make the best use of your most precious resource: *you*. Now you can truly realize your potential by performing tasks that have higher payoff values because you've set a CLEAR course for success.

CHAPTER 16
What Do I Do Next?

CHAPTER 16
What Do I Do Next?

After reading this book, you now understand:

The Who:

You

You understand that through leverage *you* can build an amazing lifestyle business from your home by bringing together "your people." You just have to be willing to step into the leadership role.

The What:

Business Model

The powerful membership-based business model that you use to bring those that you are passionate about together. Through this business model you can solve their problems and answer their needs with various products, services, and membership packages.

The Why:
Freedom

When a woman achieves financial independence, she not only experiences the healthy and positive affects of money in her own life, but she naturally shares what she knows with all those around her, which includes her family and her immediate community. When women make decisions from a place of security, they make decisions that benefit the world.

The How:
Blueprint and Tool Kit Program

You know *the who, the what, and the why.* Now I invite you to take the first step today and visit my website at www.createyourgroup.com to **learn the how**.

You can also learn more about my **Create Your Group Blueprint and Tool Kit** (and the six-month coaching program) on the following pages.

Free CD Offer
Earlier this year, I interviewed a handful of previous Create Your Group clients. If you would like a free CD of their stories where they share how they are using the Create Your Group Blueprint and Tool Kit to grow their membership-based businesses, please visit our website at www.createyourgroup.com and click the **Free CD** link.

Here's what you get in the
Create Your Membership-Based Business *Blueprint*

CHAPTER ONE
How To Create Your Group

The following is a chapter and section outline. The Blueprint contains over 4 inches of information.

Choose Your Name Carefully — Your Success Depends On It
    Educating Your Market
    Branding Big
    When To Change Your Name

Your Association Business Start-Up Timeline
    Start-up Energy
    Start-up Stress
    Checklist

What Form of Business Should You Choose for Your Association

Can You Own Your Own Association or Should You Have a Partner
    Traditional Partnerships Versus Strategic Partnerships
    Invest In Your Strategic Partnerships

How To Run a Profitable Association From Your Home Office
  Boundaries
  Office Organization
  Working Less & Making More

How To Choose Your Niche

What To Do If You Want To Change Your Niche After You Start

Avoid These Association Start-Up Mistakes
  How Many Benefits To Offer
  How To Manage The Bottom Line
  Managing The Most Important Company Asset

How To Hire Professional Advice
  Benefits
  Finding Experts

How To Choose Your Membership Benefits
  How To Focus On Member Needs
  Creating Profitable Benefits
  Running the Numbers

How To Use Focus Groups

How To Do Online Research
  Company Research
  Customer Research

How To Do Surveys
  Filtering the Feedback

How To Determine Your Pricing Structure
  Attraction with Pricing
  Niche and Structure
  Underpricing Consequences
  Mindset Pricing

CHAPTER TWO
How To Create Your Team

CHAPTER THREE
How To Create Your Leverage

CHAPTER FOUR
How To Create Your Systems

Introduction to Systems

Creating Your *Customer Service Systems*
     Virtual & Physical

Creating Your *Time Management Systems*

Creating Your *Technology Systems*

Creating Your *Member Management Systems*
     What Information Should You Collect
     The System Choices
     Strategy Planning and Reporting

Creating Your *Promotional & Lead Generation Systems*
     Website Sole Purpose
     Marketing Funnels for the Membership-Based Business
     Lead Generation Strategies-Online and Offline

Creating Your *Product & Service Development Systems*
     How To Use Infoproducts
     Where To Find Content
     What To Develop

Here's what you get in the
Create Your Membership-Based Business *Tool Kit*

SECTION ONE
Exclusive Interviews

Listen to **exclusive interviews** with **six and seven figure member-ship-based business owners**. Each interview is available on CDs and as a printed transcript.

You will learn how these **successful and exclusive entrepreneurs** below created and run their profitable membership-based businesses.

And many of them have already passed the 7-figure mark!

Milana Leshinsky, President of the Association of Coaching and Consulting Professionals on the Web
www.accpow.com

Kim Fulcher, President and CEO of Compass Life Designs
www.compasslifedesigns.com

Leslie Grossman, Co-founder of the Women's Leadership Exchange
www.womensleadershipexchange.com

Nicki Keohohou, Jane Deuber, and Gracanne Keohohou,
Co-founders of the Direct Selling Women's Alliance www.dswa.org

Dotsie Bregel, President and Founder of National Association of Baby Boomer Women
www.nabbw.com

Pat Lynch and David Barrett, CEOs and Co-owners
WomensRadio.com and WomensCalendar.org and
AudioAcrobat.com

SECTION TWO
Forms, Templates, Mind Maps and More!
(You get every tool I use to create, plan and run my associations!)

Here is the list of everything included in SECTION 2 of the tool kit and on the customer login section of our website:

- Association Business Plans
- Association Start-Up Checklist
- Teleseminar Checklist
- E-mail for New Speakers
- Speaker Agreements for Teleseminars
- Speaker Evaluations at Events
- Member Processing Checklist
- Application for Coaching Programs
- Coaching Prep Forms
- Regional Representative Kit Contents (Welcome E-mail, Guidelines and FAQs, How to Form a Writing Group Article, How To Use Biz Cards Flyer)
- Marketing Templates (Short & Long)
- Running an Association Mind map
- My Personal Rolodex (over 100 resources)
- Copies of All the Actual Promotions I Have Used Over the Last Few Years
- Cover Letter Template
- Renewal Letter Template
- Ad Samples
- Flyers
- One Page Visioning Worksheet
- One Page Business Plan
- Passion Brainstorming Worksheets
- SEO Magic
- Information Product Creation Diagram
- Information Product Launch Diagram
- And Much, Much More!

Create Your Group
Resources

Create Your Group
Resources

Article Directories (submitting your articles)
    www.ezinearticles.com
    www.ideamarketers.com
    www.goarticles.com
    www.certificate.net/wwio
    www.articlemarketer.com

Audio for Websites, Podcasting Syndication, and MP3s
    http://naww.audioacrobat.com

Blog Services
    www.blogger.com
    www.wordpress.com

Bookkeeping Software
    http://quickbooks.intuit.com

Book Printing
    www.morrispublishing.com
    www.booksjustbooks.com
    www.lulu.com

Book Publishing
    www.wymacpublishing.com
    www.parapublishing.com

Branding
    www.petermontoya.com
    www.whybrandu.com

Card Marketing
    www.bookedsolidcards.com
    www.modernpostcards.com

CD Duplication
www.wtsduplication.com
www.diskduper.com
www.infoproductguy.com
www.speakerfulfillmentservices.com
www.mimeo.com
www.polylinecorp.com

Clip Art
www.clipart.com

Coaching
Entrepreneurs - www.successconnections.com
Online Business - www.aweconnect.com
Book Publishing - www.writeyourbook.org

Copyright & Communications Law
www.legalwritepublications.com
www.copyright.gov
www.fcc.gov

Copywriting
www.wellfedwriter.com
www.redhotcopy.com
www.bly.com
www.michelepw.com

Creativity Tools
www.visualthesaurus.com
www.visual-mind.com
www.smartdraw.com (Free SmartDraw mindmapping software)

Customer Management (Database Software)
My Mail List and Address Book: OfficeDepot.com
Act by Sage – http://www.act.com
Quickbooks Customer Manager –
http://quickbooks.intuit.com/product/add_ons/customer_management.jhtml

Domain Registration and More
www.godaddy.com

Editors
angel@angelbrown.com
www.LindaJayGeldens.com

E-mail Autoresponders
www.professionalcartsolutions.com
www.aweber.com

E-mail Publishing & Marketing
www.constantcontact.com
www.professionalcartsolutions.com

E-mail Education
www.ezinequeen.com

Fax/Voicemail/E-mail (800 #)
www.onebox.com

Free Telephone Conferencing and More
www.freeconferencecall.com

Free Search Engine Submission
Open Directory Project at www.dmoz.org (The Open Directory powers the core directory services for the Web's largest and most popular search engines and portals, including Netscape Search, AOL Search, Google, Lycos, HotBot, DirectHit, and hundreds of others.)
www.About.com
www.Yahoo.com

Graphic Facilitation for Meetings
www.makemark.com

Logo Design
www.LogoYes.com
www.thelogocompany.net

Marketing
www.aweconnect.com
www.adamurbanski.com
www.actionplan.com
www.clientattraction.com
www.bookyourselfsolid.com
www.trafficschool.com

Merchant Account ($49 set-up fee waived through the NAWW/AWE)
Practice Pay Solutions - www.practicepaysolutions.com/awe
www.Paypal.com
www.Clickbank.com

Networking
www.Ryze.com
www.LinkedIn.com
www.naww.org women writers
www.aweconnect.org web entrepreneurs

Office Solutions
www.accessline.com (automated telephone system/Costco
    Discount)
www.onebox.com (fax, voicemail, and 800# all in one)
www.volusion.com (free chat software)

Office Supplies
www.officedepot.com
www.wtsmedia.com (CDs, Sleeves, Cases, etc.)

Podcast Directory Submission
Weblogs.com www.weblogs.com
Blo.gs http://blo.gs
Technorati www.technorati.com
Feed Burner www.feedburner.com/fb/a/home
Syndic8 www.syndic8.com
NewsGator www.newsgator.com/home.aspx
Feedster www.feedster.com
My Yahoo! http://my.yahoo.com
PubSub.com www.pubsub.com
Blogdigger http://blogdigger.com

BlogRolling www.blogrolling.com
BlogStreet www.blogstreet.com
Moreover http://w.moreover.com
Weblogalot http://weblogalot.com
Icerocket www.icerocket.com
News Is Free www.newsisfree.com

Publicity
www.PRWeb.com
www.anniejenningspr.com
www.publicityhound.com
www.guerrillapublicity.com

Printing
www.vistaprint.com
www.mimeo.com

Search Engine Optimization
www.overture.com
www.wordtracker.com
www.accelerateonline.net

Small Business Advice
www.startupnation.com

Survey Tool
www.surveymonkey.com
www.askdatabase.com

Transcription
http://thrivingandtranscribing.com

Virtual Team
Expert/Assistants/Programs
www.virtualteambuildingsecrets.com

For more information on the
Wyatt-MacKenzie Imprint Program
visit www.wymacpublishing.com